The Orlando Files

Sandra Renew

The Orlando Files

Poems of Dissent and Social Commentary for Performance

The Orlando Files: Poems of Dissent and Social Commentary for Performance
ISBN 978 1 76041 566 2
Copyright © text Sandra Renew 2018
Cover image: I. Sailko, CC BY-SA 3.0, https://commons.wikimedia.
org/w/index.php?curid=25095506

First published 2018 by
GINNINDERRA PRESS
PO Box 3461 Port Adelaide 5015
www.ginninderrapress.com.au

Contents

Foreword	7
Beef city	9
Will we be kind…	11
Who is giving blood for Orlando?	13
Comic	14
Pigeons know Picasso	16
Borderline	17
Using ideas as my maps	18
Plebiscite	20
Sometimes on a Wednesday	21
Face	22
Writing climate	23
River	24
Lost rivers	25
Dust storm in Melbourne 1964	26
Far oceans gyre	27
Electric	28
Everything goes back to a black and white binary	29
Frack	32
Whanganui Prayer	33
Circles protect you	34
Arms dealer	35
Transposition	36
Night bus station	37
Night bus	38
Ocean Story	40
She loves the city	41
Poster	44
It's a small town	46
Cairo photo	48

Suburbs	49
In the season of the long darkness	51
Weekend Canberra	53
After dinner	54
Definition	55
Swim	56
Bikes	57
When did she become so lonely?	58
Take one small vase of roadside flowers	59
Disquietude expatriate	60
I believe in the city	62
late evening	63
it happens overnight –	64
Refugee	65
Contemporary	66

Foreword

When I write, I rely on finding the words to create an imaginative truth. And I want this imaginative truth to say something political. In this post-truth world, our words have a new power and obligation. Now is not the time for shy words. My poetry reads best aloud, with a microphone. It appears on the page, not only for the aesthetic of the page but so it can be held up, in dim light, as the reader stands up with an audience.

I want my poetry to say something about the state of our world, this catastrophic social and environmental situation we are bringing on ourselves. So my work is social critique and revolves around dissent, contradiction, dissonance; and I write about gender, violence, war, refugees and asylum, environment and climate change. I am fascinated by the fluidity of gender, of femininities and masculinities. One of my favourite texts is *Orlando* by Virginia Woolf and it is full of the poetry of gender.

I am not trying to change the reader's mind, by preaching to the converted, but rather to record in a historical sense, to witness this most catastrophic and destructive era in human history; and most importantly, I write to keep the issues alive in the common discourse.

Beef city

I go out into the regions   away   from this cat-filled city,
places I know where they eat more beef! they're backblock
   battlers,
but they've still got time to threaten

>rape
>castrate
>spay you
>like a no-good heifer.

I'm not here to settle old scores,
the *run-her-out of-town* history's a territory of memory –
>*jackaroos-bash-the-dykes*
>*pub-night-Friday,*
>*drinking on the highway.*

beef city is a place to test the legislation,
a place to run the plebiscite, the will of the nation, find the
   free-speech, no-harm threshold
tap into discussions held in every household

here in the dust of the beef-focused city,
a bridal party stands up to marry, lesbians are seen here, faces
   in the shadows –
this place of sacred vows
>is the place where you all vote.

I know I'm a dragon in your cat-filled city
I know my frown and fire scares the marble from your beef,
   in my high rider boots and flash waistcoat
there are no grooms here, no room to normalise your hate.

I know I'm a dragon in your cat-filled city
and all across the country we are waiting for your vote, I
   know you are afraid of unleashing pride and difference
there's no room here to normalise your hate.

we don't need a plebiscite, a vote, to divide and label us.
we need the politicians to stand and defend us.
we just want equality, change the drift of history
we don't need a plebiscite, excuse to raise your hate.

I am a dragon in your dusty cities
a dragon breathing fire, melting asphalt on your streets
will the beef-eating people and the cat-filled cities
stand up and call it when we hear the words of hate?

realistically speaking I'll never be on a turned back boat
but I'm a dragon breathing fire, a dragon breathing smoke
I want the politicians to hands up vote.

don't give the hate-sayers reason to harm
accept me as dragon whose time has come –
accept me as a dragon…

Will we be kind…

I've seen families make a home under a piece of blue plastic
when tyrants and madmen try to empty a land of its people –
I've seen the ordered German mind thrown into confusion
by the open heart and open hands of Merkel –
it is a talked about thing, it is not difficult, knowing who
 cries out.

when we have everything, we want something more,
and in panic, we control our borders with Border Force –
I worry about the necessity
of generosity in kindness – and our inability to step up

will we love when we are thirsty?
will we be kind when we flee?
when our shelter is gone, will we be just?
who will give us sanctuary?

I've seen families destroy their children in the season of Mardi
 Gras
when the street is a theatre for coming out – the inhumanity of
the pink triangle and the cruelty of the black haunts me still –
my body was written on the Nazi's chart of stigma and since I
 have known this
I have also known that the darkness has already approached
 and settled –

this is how time passes, the words to hate us are still there –
in fear, we close ourselves in, inside black silence
I worry about the necessity
of generosity in kindness – and that you will kill us with your
 hatred –

will we be loved when we are thirsty?
will we find kindness when we flee?
when our shelter is gone, will we be treated justly?
who will give us sanctuary?

Who is giving blood for Orlando?

Gay Pride Month in Orlando
brings the kiss
and then, closely following,
the hate crime
the guns –
gays and Latinos are stitched together by hate and guns

the viewing public struggles with overlays of terrorist attack,
    homophobia, race and gender – who will give their blood
    for the players?

all currency, including hate, settles in its place of origin.
    remittance dollars find their way home. it's Latin Night at
    the Pulse –
hate came in with him on the darkness. we will deny him his
    name but not respond with hate –
let him take it with him

Note: When I look through the web sites for statistics on gun
massacres in the United States, (the mass shooting tracker, the
visual guide to mass shootings, the gun violence archive)…can you
imagine the obscenity of such normalised atrocity, atrocity of such
magnitude that a web industry is generated…I find that 164 days
into 2016 – that is, by June – there had been 133 mass shootings (of
four or more deaths).
In some areas of the United States of America homosexuals are
prohibited from donating blood.

Comic

it starts as a comic strip novel
with violent colour and *booms* and *bams* and catastrophic impacts
making us all less civil –
the signs tacked above the fish and chippy bar
are not portending luck so far

we strive to provide
a welcoming environment:
for hatred, here, there is no tolerance –

no head-butts, no harassment,
no 'cut her face with broken glass' –
no conversation inflammation

*

he wins by a Twitter, so now
straight white men rule
in a post-truth Trump(led) crowd

*

our frisson of fear disturbs the streets
we are falling in the wake of Queer
in Sydney's west, we're not safe here

for lovers' quest or marrying queer,
hitching up with a Q
a rainbow novel exploding clear,

just so you know, we are not fooled
straight white men have always ruled

it's the gay panic defence, the smell and essence
of William Burrough's shocking *Queerness* –

it scares the Trumps so queerly
a lost line of hypocrisy, an awkwardness of lonely

*

in the predatory streets,
Twitter affected no-brain clowns
breathless with adrenalin

hidden haters' hoodies disguising
chalking up a poofter bashing
high fiving, gay hating –

bloody sound of *bams* and *bangs*
crushed cheekbones faces slashed
no unlikely risings from the dead…

Note: Gay panic (and trans panic) defence is a legal defence usually against charges of assault or murder, where the assaulter claims violent temporary insanity because of being in unexpected proximity to a gay or transgender person.

Pigeons know Picasso

we do whatever we have to do to get ourselves through,
to save the horses
dismount, walk along side, encourage with soft tongue clicks –
we listen carefully to the river, watch machines grinding
    pigment –
I know what you know…colour is sound-frequency vibration
trapped in its tube, closed in its tin, pure red yellow blue,
    pure rainbow

pigeons know Picasso
bees know a Monet when they see one

it's knowing when to light the match
flicking it into the current won't illuminate the water,
but, it might ignite the water –

the machine grinds on,
colours are the grit of the earth and we can no longer make
    out the rock
they came from

Borderline

another take on it
   is taking it on
   taking it further
         gender bending
         cross dressing

she likes a piece of it
   pirating man-things
   waistcoat and pipes
         Bowie cheekbones
         frisson androgyny

my Radclyffe Hall, my George Eliot
   disguise and drag, taboo
   walk the gender walk
         swap a wedding dress
         for an art tattoo

Notes: George Eliot was Mary Anne Evans.
Orlando is a fabulous Virginia Woolf novel about the fluidity and ephemerality of gender. Today we know Orlando as the site of a gay hate crime, one of one of the biggest gun massacres in the United States in 2016.

Using ideas as my maps

(from 'My Back Pages', Bob Dylan)

if you want to know what blue I mean
it's the blue, stoned aloneness of Dylan.

if you want to know what road I see
it's the lost, cold-stone, lonely road of Dylan

   clean despair from under my fingernails
   save my skin, my tattoos and blunted needles,
   confront my body piercing and sharp soul

if you want to know what I saw from the sixties
it's the cold blue-stone, lonely heart of Dylan

   dry my feet from the rising ocean
   dust them on a crust of dry sand, splint
   my broken bones with over-heated sunlight –

if you want to know how a poem turns to music
it's the hard and harried harmonica of Dylan

keep the old fear from my body
   seduce me with a coat of guitar and whiskey
   a prophet sings: youth sees a messiah

if you want to know what blue I mean
it's the blue, stoned cold aloneness of Dylan.

   war will kill us: we knew a warning when we heard it
   hard rain falls on all the blue-eyed sons
   for this prophet, there are no dead lines

if you want to know what blue I mean
it's the blue-stoned aloneness of Dylan.

if you want to know what blue I mean
it's the blue, stoned aloneness of Dylan.

Note: Bob Dylan was awarded the Nobel Prize for Literature 2016. The award provoked intense debate about the nature of poetry and song, and the worth of Dylan's work regarding merit for a literature award. This poem is written in defence of Dylan.

Plebiscite

We were so close to a law that promised us equality…
Just before morning, before the dawn sky
I saw the source of the river.
Weeks later I paddled, exhausted, through the delta islands.
Do you even know what you want from me?

*

You keep raising red herrings, issues that are sidebars, irrelevant to anything important…
Wiping sauce from the plate
with bread, hot this morning
he tells me there was a moment when he thought he was a lesbian.
Not even his house mates came to the house-warming.

*

Life is hard enough, you are running us ragged, how much compromise is required for fitting in?
What kind of joke are you in?
My jeans are urban black and cool,
the city is no flowing river, it's a chaos of traffic,
confusion, preference, and the possibility of the noise of guns.

Note: In Australia in 2016 we came within a fingernail of legislated marriage equality. This poem is about why we stopped holding our breath…

Sometimes on a Wednesday

sometimes on a Wednesday I look for public poetry
as it flutters in a place where the lines don't join up neatly
and the colours bleed between into a space
that is not words…

sometimes on a Wednesday
we come to read the poetry
which weathers and leaches
letters into litter…

sometimes on a Wednesday without changing anything
I look for words that startle as they hang on public walls
collaged on the noticeboards, pasted onto fences
that are broken…

a palimpsest of protest
the words are changing everything
the litter and the garbage
is transcended by the poetry

Note: Written for Bill poetries project in the 2016 Canberra Noted Festival.

Face

Hands to the sky, palms upwards under the slow drip of
   leaking clouds –
I catch warm rain mixed with tears, on skin colder than steel.

I miss my country
I miss the weight of fear
and death
I look for colour and light
that cannot be seen here

Cartoonists draw blasphemy that shocks, journalists mock
   and laugh at power –
if I resign the front line the killers will come for me.
   Democracy is built on this…

thumbnail moon
gleams red before
the sunrise
then leaches to silver
with the last dregs of my coffee

Writing climate

the colour purple
a new, extreme
weather warning
arrow climbs green, yellow, red –
plan ahead for purple

in poetic cartography, unknown poets map the progress
of love and loss and longing – she pins their poems on the
noticeboard, traces words with her fingertips from first
appearance, skipping over line breaks and pauses, em-dash
and indrawn breath, until the meaning blazes

record the world
with a cold pen, or burn it
with indifference
am I more than a witness
to the Earths destruction?

the trees, carbon trading underground, resource sharing
amongst themselves to keep the planet going…

paperbark swamp
library of record
growth rings
preserved under mud
I see no urban gods

River

indigenous nations' conversation on the river –
our country is not as it should be
flat plains are lost flood plains of a lost river,
skeletons of river-red-gum forests where old growth trees
    were strangled
by regulated creeks and raw-banked sculpture of irrigation
    channels
and drowned river bays.
Blood of warring warriors thickens Pink Lake
dams cry out, dry out, where they should not be...
pumps grind screaming in drought-dry water levels,
intake pipes hang in mid-air,
salt rises, raw sand-mining dunes blow in dust storms,
    sediment drops on muddy water,
wetlands turned drylands uncover mussel-shell middens
embedded in red soil banks far from where they should be...
Ngarrindjeri, Ngarkat, Wiradjuri, Yorta Yorta, Mutti Mutti,
Wamba Wamba, Barapa Barapa, Murrumbidgee, Murray,
Darling, Yellowin, Coorong, Koondrook, Perricoota,
Chowilla, Wallpolla –
people   indigenous conversation protecting country

after burn
scrub habitat reduced
to skeleton
who is the arsonist
and how many deaths?

Note: A response evoked from the book: *Murray River Country – An Ecological Dialogue With Traditional Owners* by Jessica K. Weir.

Lost rivers

water is our body-blood, our kinship, our survival
   when the invaders built a City,
   when they entombed a river
   it was shocking to my body
it all became political

I consigned it to my memory –
   when the river disappeared
   the river words were gone –
all are beyond retrieval
   unless we remember
incantation brings revival
   when the City buries the river
   even when I lose my body

        Tank Stream
        Wu-gan-ma-gul-ya Creek
        Brickfields Creek
        Darling Harbour Creek
        Black Wattle Swamp Creek
        Wests Creek
        Palmers Creek…

Dust storm in Melbourne 1964

rain system
radar shows green and black
enormous swirling
finger print of climate –
should we have seen it coming?

Erosion changes the topsoil, moves it from one level of earth to the next. Water works itself out of the soil, then disappears. Earth cracks and dries until the willy-willy spins the dust, moves it to stain the air, then chokes the oxygen from it. In the city on the southern edge of the continent, dust banks cloud and roll, billow, settle on buildings and bitumen, clouding windows, roughening soft asphalt like sandpaper, gagging mouths, making our noses bleed with the scraping. We roll the grit of dust on the enamel of our teeth, our bodies shudder with its foreignness. It's earth, out of place and out of time. Earth to dust, and moving –

this city running on time
empties time of meaning
empties colour of purpose
empties place of reason…
my delusions are written on a fantail wrapper

Far oceans gyre

shipping containers float and bob
alongside sumo-sized jelly fish –
movement masses in the far oceans

twenty foot of standardised economic units
rises and turns on the rhythmic swing and surge –
primitive life feeds on unplanned by-products

both are out-puts of a world gone to greed
past common-sense and credibility –
unexpected consequences, entirely foreseeable

Electric

Yesterday, when my balloon was losing air, I knew I could
hold out for so long and no more –
the world tips, balance becomes un balance. Will I too
become a refugee from the heating of the earth, the violence
of the storm, contamination of water courses, drying rivers?
Although we say everyone matters, with turned back boats
we have nothing to gain. We can refuse to panic but Tampa,
Nauru, and Manos are only the first of the lies – north moves
west. South moves towards us.

night flight
a million pricks of light
over India
each village, electric light
coal power heating the earth

Everything goes back to a black and white binary

everything goes back
   to a black
   and white binary
yes/no   on/off   0/1 –
as their pools dry up
it's goodbye platypus
you're here, then you're lost –

somebody is building an island
of crowd-sourced fact-checks
a madness of Wikipedia
post-truth,
   alternative truths
   any truth is true
education is a dirty
   word –

a madness with no method
is stood up against a wall
monotremes are for extinction
islands are a new, truth fixation
yes/no   on/off   0/1 –
they're here, then they're lost –

afterwards
when four-hundred and thirty-eight cubic feet of air
we breathe in every day
knocks us under with the weight and
more than our share
of microbes, gas, grit, dust and more
   detritus
we know our use-by date is closing on us

sing hallelujah
with our hats pulled down and our eyes closed –
sing an anthem for a planet –
if this is the case, however we see it
sometimes a happening completely destroys us
   we *are* detritus
the universe expands and goes on without us

not for us the Greenies, rabbiting on
about the hidden life of trees,
sophisticated complicated silent language
   electrical impulse
   of smell and taste –
not for us the hydrothermal magic
at the bottom of the ocean
or gravitational energy waves

everything goes back to a black and white binary
yes/no   on/off   0/1 –
as their pools dry up
it's goodbye platypus
you're here, then you're lost –

madness with no method
stands up against a wall
monotremes are for extinction
islands become the new truth fixation
yes/no   on/off   0/1 –
they're here, then they're lost –

Frack

I will never map a new country
never raise a flag to claim 'unboundaried' land
and now I've seen the water burn –

a match ignites the soft creek flow,
gas flames alight from open taps
the taste of water in my glass makes my stomach churn –

I've seen a moonscape of destroyed plains with rigs and tanks,
escaping gas, simmering evaporation pools,
where grasslands once gave big roos a nesting place –

I've seen grown men in suits lie to us
as we buy our water bottled from a global store

they think we are not watching them,
we weren't born yesterday, they say –
but their fracking only started here fracking yesterday

old country turned into dead country –
there are places where the water burns
I've seen the tap flow ignited, the creek lit up by one match

Note: Fracking (hydraulic fracturing): the process of injecting liquid at high pressure into subterranean rocks and boreholes to force open existing fissures and extract oil or gas. This process includes injecting known toxic chemicals into the fracking water to lubricate the drill bit. These toxic chemicals contaminate the aquifers from which creek and river waters flow and into which wells are sunk for drinking water. Millions of gallons of water are needed to successfully frack natural gas from shale deposits.

Whanganui Prayer

River!
we pledge a vow of compassion to every bend and
waterway and lagoon, current and fall,
you stand as a citizen, your legal voice
must save your water –
for what is more extreme than a river
deprived of water?

Forest!
human beings should not be seeing this –
four-hundred-year-old tree chopped down and
transported to a wild life corridor
to make a home for native refugees –
for what is more unforgivable
than old sediment of old attitudes?

Earth!
we know you despair of us!
your persona as Tree, your legal standing as River,
your named Identity –
for what is more unforgivable
than human beings
making you fight us on our terms?

Circles protect you

Circles protect you if you let them – who hasn't seen you
dancing in the dark? It's our turn to give the circle protection

Shanghai Yangtze River mudflats
were a haven on the migration path –
Australia China Korea Russia and back again,
our birds circle and circle, back again.

In polluted skies they circle and circle where the mudflats were
once a landing place. When the mangroves and sandbanks
are taken, the circle is broken. Extending protection of
development exemptions, we circle in red tape objections

birds circle south, north, and back again
homeless birds, refugees
dying out…extinction

Arms dealer

how is it that the truth always rests with the minority, with
those who have an opinion, who have nothing to lose?
how is it that there is so much poetry of old men and dead
poets…that it has so much weight and so little truth?
how is it that we have become, with a deft sleight of politics
and strategic change in wording, unremarked, a country
excelling in the manufacture of arms, war materiél?
why are we the ones to raise our voices, to make a link
between making arms, selling arms, and killing those we love?
guns and shoes
massacres and refugees
today's icons
with shooters, fishers, farmers

places of the mass shootings and gun massacres, names we knew in romance, and in the songs we sang together – Lesbos, Orlando, Baton Rouge, Nice, Paris, there are others – are belled now, sounding sadness, salted, and bitter, strange forces test their strength, crazy minds of misfits, misogynists, the criminally insane, look for ways to join…

Transposition

warlords plotted the poet's murder –
how does she separate from family?
by leaving herself –
she finds herself in a room
how does she know the room?
she knows it by the blood on the floor

the poet lets her pistol fall…

when you can't be sure of your country,
who is at home in your homeland?

you're a mark on the landscape
you exist outside vertical space
there are places here that are important to all of us –
you will find her with her hands in the earth

still she lives surrounded by strangers…

the son washes café dishes with Persian poetry,
Iranian pop songs –
his poet mother serves food
at home in a new country

following the contours to improve on what she brings
she puts herself, somehow, into a landscape
pointing up soft lines with rounded rock
marking out a circle, marking a spot with an inside and an outside
where none has been –
marking the earth as hers, with stones

Night bus station

1 departures

buses lined up like caterpillars digesting the garden,
waiting for metamorphosis into night-infatuated moths
    insatiable,
wanting more…
drivers eating again crumbs falling on shirt fronts
excessive tomato sauce to make a pie more palatable,
wanting more…
uniform shirts straining
over sedentary bellies
international students, outsize bags spilling open taking in
    more
coming and going
electronic manifest scrolling ticketless travel
children using the empty space for impromptu ballet
embracing the polished unclean floor
in screaming practice

2 waiting in arrivals

six year old swings feet flicks hair
and it falls like a shroud –
balances on the backs of the seats
arms outstretched, voice-shrieks high above the conversation
    and
rumble of wheelie bags – *look at me*
she can fall either into the glass window
or into the path of the moving buses

Night bus

1 sandwiches in brown paper

there's the bus station for the night bus
there's waiting and reading the tiny screen and repacking
there's sandwiches in brown paper
there's warm soft drink in crushable, rip-top cans
there's eating, unwrapping, repacking
there's last minute instructions, boarding announcements
there's repacking, eating, luggage-wheeling
scrabbling through bags and suitcases and repacking
there's greeting and hugging and handshaking
and queueing and repacking and eating
there's ticket buying, and ticket rereading, and ticket finding and losing
and repacking on the run and finding the bus and checking which window
and phoning and texting and scrolling
there's announcement listening and queueing and boarding and waving goodbye

roast beef sandwich
yesterday's white bread and last week's mayo
mustard and tangy cheese
he's driving through the night
bus full of silent passengers

2 boarding

you're just a girl in red and black, hands closed over your face
waiting, leaning, outside the bus, beside the queue
inside, the driver's console is dark, unattended
the seats are filling up and you are not moving
the window behind you, past you, opens up the street outside
why do you wait in the space between?

our overnight bus reflects in the panel behind you
windscreen wiper arms held together like hands in prayer
or a judgemental parent waiting for explanation

3 hiding in our uniforms

look at us lining up for our photo in blue uniform shirts
we're a bit smug because we're good civic citizens
going to a conference dressed neat and clean
shiny in our haircuts and arm folded pride
we're not even noticing the anarchy around us –
behind us the buildings burn, men in smoked uniforms blast
   in the windows
children starve and beg, widows are cast out and cast off
their bruises livid neon-lit warnings that the world is not right
our blameless hands are clasped behind us now,
our shirts still pressed and clean, pristine

Ocean Story

raising the shimmering barriers and rejecting the corpses of
global warming argument – what curious fringes of resistance
surge when we deploy the sea defences! The propaganda does
sound ugly...

shearwaters
know nothing of the politics
of climate change
but they are on the front line...
death by plastic in the ocean

the Pacific Ocean is where thermonuclear weapons have been
tested, our bell wether for changing weather – and is the
origin of carefree wave-gliding.
tracks made by supertankers as they criss-cross this ocean,
east west, west east, are marked by non-weather-related
clouds, allowing the paths to be surveilled by satellites...this
cloud messes with the climate.

forty degrees Celsius
wind from the north-west
I miss
the slow drip
of leaking clouds

She loves the city

she loves the safety of the city   where she can lose herself
    and you
in a crowd of clowns performing tragedy and comedy –
in the obscurity of the city   as a target   she's one of many

her name is never known   and the faces that she lives in
    are anonymous and closed

but the ideas, the ideas come to her like oxygen
she's free to argue   her dissent and shocked amazement
invading armies can be defeated   but new ideas can't be
    blocked
or abandoned or resisted

scream her name scream her name scream her name

*

she loves the city   but when she crosses to the regions
    you can see her!
at midnight mark her door with expletives and paint
scratch her car   with broken bottles

scream her name scream her name scream her name

you can follow her   down the one street   out
onto an empty highway   where what is done is personal
    and has no name
just a pub lunch wink and nudge,   crazy eyes alcoholic
    mouth

so far away from ocean   you're afraid   of what you
   think you see
washed up from across the sea
you allow your isolation   to distil hatred   you protect
   yourself with distance

in your one-street town   on the edge of town   desert is
   encroaching
buildings generally collapsing   sand degrading paddocks
makes a dune maze   with cattle tracks

leading from all points   to one small pump and trough

you think of outside as two days to the east and the coast
you know inside as sporadic fan and coughing generator
even here with dial-up internet   social media vomits hate mail

facebook friends could post from anywhere   who graffiti's
   hate-speech?

gays still have a sickness, climate change is a conspiracy –
where One Nation is the answer, dissent is a suspicion
where a gun is a right for lifestyle protection

normal is the question,

scream her name scream her name scream her name

*

she loves the safety of the city   where she can lose herself
    and you
in a crowd of clowns performing tragedy and comedy –
in the obscurity of the city   as a target   she's one of many

her name is never known   and the faces that she lives in
    are anonymous and closed

to this there is no come back   unless she comes back to
    the city
nothing here is personal,   she's one among the millions
she's safe here   in her namelessness   free to be inside
    her city

she loves the city   that does not know her   on the edge
    of ocean
that delivers space and light

Poster

what cards do I hold?
I know how it ends, I know how we got here –
can you remember how it started?

now, when actually means not really and literally means really
I have alternative facts, I've misled and forgotten
but accurate or not, being found out changes everything

which stories are true? we know how it came up
and how it went down – we both knew the poster of Angela
    Davis
light absorbed into the black halo of Afro

it's knowing you're a short haired woman –
it's what I know about the activities of such women
how I can't deny that my body recoils at the scent of gun-oil
    on your hands

the dark grease of well-handled metal under your nails
warning whiff of gunpowder as you shrug off your jacket
it's knowing it's not a mouse gun that pulls your pocket out
    of shape

it's reading later there was a target and who used her body as
   a shield
who carried the assault rifle and who loaded and sighted the
   weapon
who carried the telltale residual weight of metal bullet casings,

unrolling the old poster – what cards do we hold, really?

Note: *Time* magazine, week of 31 August 1970 – Black Panther
activist Angela Davis eludes the FBI following the murder of
California Judge Harold J. Haley. Davis is suspected of the slaying
and of taking part in an armed courtroom invasion to free the
Soledad Three, three black convicts on trial for killing a guard at
Soledad State Prison.
Mouse guns are small handguns that are easy to conceal, but hard
to use accurately. While exact definitions can vary, they are generally
considered to be the smallest handguns that still retain practical value.

It's a small town

it's a small town, a nice town, Tidy Town
it keeps itself nice
street-side rubbish collection, trim lawns,
artesian sourced sprinklers

it's a helping-hand town, a friendly town, inclusive town
it shares itself
Men's Shed, RV-friendly signage,
freshly spruced   public conveniences

it's an independent town, an up-itself town, a Big Something town
it shows itself off
Annual Gymkhana, *Open Historic House* days
Running of the Rams town

it's a highway town, a no-visible-means-of-support town
a don't-blink-or-you'll-miss-it town
closed-down Chicken Factory, empty silo, drive-in   drive-out
a no-reason-to-stop-here town

*

they are small-town girls, nice girls, Dux of high school,
    Banana Queen girls
they keep themselves nice
knees together, done their homework, ironed their uniforms
    nice girls
they kiss chastely in the tuckshop, nice-ly

they are get-on-the-bus-to-the-City girls, Schoolies Week at
   the Gold Coast girls
looking for dykes who are nice
girls-helping-their-grandmas type dykes, June Dally Watkins
   deportment class dykes
bus-ticket-back-to-the-small-town dykes

steer away from the bike dykes, the tattoos and overalls,
   body-piercing tough dykes,
eschew the bad-language, gum chewing, pavement spitting,
   graffiti-writing not-nice dykes
the wouldn't-be-seen-dead-in-our-home-town dykes –

small-town-girls-in-the-Big-City dykes
look for vegetarian, mantra humming, vanilla dykes
who all came to the city from nice towns dykes
hook up with consciousness-raising, massage giving, L-Word
   bingeing dykes

let's-go-to-our-High-School-Reunion-nice dykes

Cairo photo

Write for rights, take action, send a letter. Can words against repression secure freedom?
Three years on, more lost birthdays, more words. Words incarcerate him…will words ever release him?

Cairo bloodbath
Shawkan takes a picture
captures a crackdown –
another birthday
in Tora prison

Suburbs

in the suburbs of the city, on the outskirts of the centre
on the cul-de-sacs and boulevards
that stretch for miles and miles,
in the shopping centres,
chemist, fish and chips, supermarket, deli trendy,
the takeaway is discontent with plenty…

and fear of missile strikes, an undercurrent frisson of uncertainty
from North Korea's madness and depravity
and US presidential dementia and immaturity…

*

in the suburbs of the city
a horizon flashing neon, allows a partial resolution,
tattoos are frowned upon unless they're 'hood ID,

the moon is hanging over on the ordinary, so ordinary,
all this becomes so ordinary,
mundane yet interlaced with drama over overweight
with too much weight
on infilling the green space, and tall poppy lopping…

*

underlay and overlay of carpets, and the pelmets and the drapery,
takes our time and energy
when we're needed in the polity
to vote for gays and water-flow and stand against a push
that will make Australia lead the world
producing hardware for the military

*

in the suburbs of the city, on the outskirts of the centre,
where the house price war is crowded for the houses so ordinary,
the lattes and the lawnmowers
soothe our frisson of uncertainty

In the season of the long darkness

In the season of the long darkness there will be a hundred poems
about the ice shelf cracking free, stories of A68 seceding from
 Larson C...

this newly calved iceberg the size of a small country, a parallel
 dimension away
from the blood-and-soil nationalism we know here as
 democracy –

but my memory is of the cold: Celsius, minus twenty-eight
 degrees,
and of cold imagined eye-blinding dazzle in sea jewels and sea
 ice diamonds
and I remember the blue: a turquoise sea, blue bergs, blue
 sheet ice,   Blue Whale song, and flares going off from
 Casey Station

*

another Universe away, the sun sets before five and rises after
 seven, machine-politics in big cities make the idea of money,

musicians mend instruments and festival goers sit into the
 night
blanketed in electric warmth, hearing our winter myths and
 stories...

we're wired-in to catastrophic politics and pod-casts from
 America,
it's the age of LED lights and we're lit by blinking modems

*

so quietly, our newest country bobs and floats,
free to make itself in Antarctica's image

or, in silence on our airwaves, melt and disappear,
in blue, and turquoise, and crystal jewels and diamonds

Note: Inspired by blog posts by Australian Antarctic Division science reporter Dr Wendy Pyper as she joined scientists on a seven-week voyage to the sea ice zone off East Antarctica in 2012.

Weekend Canberra

he drives his Nissan Pulsar like it is a Jeep Cherokee –
revs it on the roundabouts, does donuts in the cul-de-sacs
at midnight on a weeknight…

from a roadside pickup pile he finds a mattress with an
 unobtrusive watermark
where in normal circumstance a large established stain
of uncertain but certainly disreputable heritage shouts sleaze
 from the centre…

slips through the Summer Nats' street parade on Northbourne
gives the finger to the driver with last-minute brakes on
his souped up flashy chrome and noise…

thumbs up to the wet T-shirt girl steaming, posturing…

on Monday he coaxes a ladybird beetle onto his same finger-
 for-fingering
and carries her to a wind-burned leaf in a bottlebrush tree out
 of the way
of workman's boots and mates spewing last night's fun-time
 into the garden mulch

After dinner

after dinner –
   the crowded loneliness of a lost road.
   like wind on my face another world comes to me,
   citric pucker of lost hope,
   forgotten jewels
   and the 'so last century' sound of coins jingling in my pocket

– a door closes with the relief of guests departing

Definition

sometimes a word comes along, over centuries, that is so fantastically appropriate for the times, so opportunistically opportune, that it is imperative to look it up!

over Hiroshima
birds in flight ignite –
a word
sounds the world –
kakistocracy

Note: A kakistocracy is a state or country run by the worst, least qualified or most unscrupulous citizens. The word was coined as early as 1600.

Swim

She learned to swim in the Moorabool. Saggy, elastic, hand-me-down bathers, feet pushing off from the black mud bank or the small sand island in the middle of the current. Nose and mouth and eyes full of tea-dark river. Her sister, apparently a 'natural', watches smirking, while she sinks and flails and chokes.

chlorinated concreted,
lane marked, fifty-yard pools
Dawn Fraser
swimming for Australia
all still to come

Bikes

they take their time entering the new city, ostentatiously
slowing to the speed limit
inked insignia on faded denim, jeans torn, detailing
embroidered with a line from Cohen...*like a bird on a wire*

scuffed boots, soles worn where they've taken the weight of
stopping and starting from P plate to upgrade, Northbourne
Avenue filleted by the raw, new railway...
now a single line of throbbing CCs, rumbling revs, parades
their menace and my insignificance –

I'm reflected in her helmet visor for a moment when she
slows for the lights, the one hundred bikes crowd in beside
her before sweeping on
I want to be here for the end of it

When did she become so lonely?

she was ten when she learned to drive a Model T Ford,
converted to carry farm tools and hay bales, daggy sheep,
shovels, and wire-cutters, spare rolls of plain and barbed wire,
pieces of harness for various sized saddle horses –
all the grit of blowing sand

she still drives the track following directions her father shouts
into the wind as she moves off, slow-riding the clutch, stop,
start, break open the bales, sling the slabs onto the sheep
track, a hillside of movement as sheep string out along the
hay line.

she knows the sign at the crossroads – Population 23. she's
been to the city, a dual highway of impatience, no one stops
for anyone. she's been away to school, seen a new world. she's
come back.

check the level in the dam, the intake pipe still under water,
start the pump, open the tank, clear the trough.
cracking clay at the waterline stinks in the drying sun, wet
cloying mud a false barrier along the yellow edge.
crows keep their distance, keep their eye in. all they need is
patience.

Take one small vase of roadside flowers

take one small vase of roadside flowers
pick it up from the floor out of the way of crushing boots
replace it on the packing crate table
let it sit in the silence of the empty shipping container
let the small plastic truck, stable enough on three wheels, sit
    beside the vase
let the concussive boom of big guns, rattle of AK 47s, the
    grenades, the IEDs
come closer, vibrate the metal walls,
expend itself on nothing –
let the empty room wait

Disquietude expatriate

Using the time between the here and the there, while she
    wonders if there is a there-there,
present and past make a lost future, turn the time between
into the here,

bring the past to the lost future – when you're knocked down
    you stand up.
she is unsure just who the barbarians are in this country…

It is the season of heavy fog
when all the familiar things she thought were etched clearly
    on stone
are blurred and made sinister, disappearing and reappearing
    as mist swirls and settles,
while she waits for an unreliable midday sun to burn through
    grounded cloud.
All is apprehendable.

All she knows is the pure comprehension of moisture drops
lining the underside of branches high into the unfamiliar tree,
liquid, constant, until the uncertain light eventually absorbs
    them into atmosphere.

It's something she sees – no language, no words give it form
    or reduce its power
to punch her guts breathless
it's something she knows – no touch, no embrace gives it a
    reason to step back from her reach,
a circle drawn in dust

It's something she became, foreign – a stranger, an alien to herself,
she sends texts she is not sure of to her mother who cannot read
in a language she hears as noise

The day she is not overwhelmed by the plug-in appliances,
this day creeps up on her –
but even this day she mishears the request from her daughter
in her new language *I want to do art and craft classes*
not *I want to go to after-school care*

I believe in the city

I believe in the city and the infinite power it holds to fix things…

every fourteen days when earth and moon and sun align
a spring tide reaches higher

every January and June when Earth comes closest to the sun
a King tide reaches higher

every eighteen point six years when Earth and Moon orbit planes realign
a Tidal Epoch reaches higher

we blame without fixing…
El Niños and La Niña's episodic variations come top of mind

the ocean reaches higher
with two degrees warming, four point seven metres sea rising,
two hundred and eighty million in world cities underwater
the ocean will reach us

with two degrees warming, four point seven metres sea rising
six hundred and sixty-eight thousand Australian coastal people
will find the ocean reaching us

today is not a new dawn,
an unusual reality check is not needed –
a new fact set, unnecessary –
tidal maps and temperature records, rain gauges give us the numbers

I believe in the city and the infinite power we hold to fix things

Note: *Climate change could lead to massive sea rises* Tom Arup and Robert Crawford, *South Coast Register*, 6 August 2017.
Tide in Wikipedia.

late evening

when I arrive home
your bicycle
leans askew
on the veranda post

it happens overnight –

we know from the brittleness
of nineteen thirty-six
when people turn on each other
it's a warning

Refugee

the ocean is between us
and yet today in the full heat of the white glare
I know with a certainty you cannot shake
that I could cross that ocean
tasting salt and blood
crawl, finally, up on to the sand of your country
walk the beaches until I find you

Contemporary

for me, there is a trick to it,
the meaning of life, angst and sturm –

it's radio news –
I'm informed but not quite terrified

on Google maps I measure with thumb and finger protractor
the distance between Korea and the US eastern coast, Darwin
and Korea,

note that the 'testing' is again today and tabled options and
some opinions
are, broadly speaking, stop talking, keep talking,

and 'don't make me come up there' a bedtime threat
before the lights go out

www.ingramcontent.com/pod-product-compliance
Lightning Source LLC
Chambersburg PA
CBHW062157100526
44589CB00014B/1864